Karsten "Ted" Aschenbrandt

THE PERFECT
SAUSAGE

Making and Preparing Homemade Sausage

D1227435

Schiffer Publishing Ltd

4880 Lower Valley Road • Atglen, PA 19310

Other Schiffer Books on Related Subjects:

Pure Steak, 978-0-7643-3927-1, $29.99

Pure BBQ, 978-0-7643-4013-0, $24.99

Copyright © 2013 by Schiffer Publishing, Ltd.

Originally published as *Das Perfekte Würstchen: Selbst Wusten, Grillen, Rezepte mit Wurst* by HEEL Verlag GmbH. Translated from German by Ingrid Elser

Photos: Thomas Schultze
Cover photos: Thomas Schultze, Stockfood (bottom row, middle image)
Layout and design: Claudia Renierkens, renierkens kommunications-designs, Köln
Foodstyling: Christine Birnbaum

Library of Congress Control Number: 2013930300

Cover design adaptation by Bruce M. Waters
Layout design adaptation by Mark David Bowyer
Type set in Futura Hv BT / Futura Bk BT

ISBN: 978-0-7643-4302-5
Printed in China

Schiffer Publishing's titles are available at special discounts for bulk purchases for sales promotions or premiums. Special editions, including personalized covers, corporate imprints, and excerpts can be created in large quantities for special needs. For more information, contact the publisher.

Published by Schiffer Publishing, Ltd.
4880 Lower Valley Road
Atglen, PA 19310
Phone: (610) 593-1777; Fax: (610) 593-2002
E-mail: Info@schifferbooks.com

For our complete selection of fine books on this and related subjects, please visit our website at www.schifferbooks.com. You may also write for a free catalog.

This book may be purchased from the publisher. Please try your bookstore first.

We are always looking for people to write books on new and related subjects. If you have an idea for a book, please contact us at proposals@schifferbooks.com

In Europe, Schiffer books are distributed by
Bushwood Books
6 Marksbury Ave.
Kew Gardens
Surrey TW9 4JF England
Phone: 44 (0) 20 8392 8585; Fax: 44 (0) 20 8392 9876
E-mail: info@bushwoodbooks.co.uk
Website: www.bushwoodbooks.co.uk

Karsten "Ted" Aschenbrandt

THE PERFECT
SAUSAGE

Making and Preparing Homemade Sausage

CONTENTS

Let's Talk about *Sausage*

The sausage is a part of almost every culture and cuisine in which meat is fried or grilled. A barbecue without sausages...simply unthinkable, and the stadium, county fair, or amusement park would only be half the fun without some form of sausage.

Sausages have also been faithful companions at the kitchen table for decades, and in my neighborhood there are only a few people who grew up without sausages.

I know people who prefer a good fried or grilled sausage over a piece of meat and I fully understand this. Unfortunately, not every sausage is as good as the links available at the butchers of yore—or like the ones we ate on vacation, or those of Uncle Heinz. Almost everybody has a nostalgic sausage experience: the memory of an incomparable taste. So why not make sausages yourself? It is much easier than you think, and the decision about what goes inside the casings, how thick, how long, and how fine the sausages ought to be lies with the sausage maker alone. The possibilities are unlimited and who else brings handmade sausages to a cook out? Just seeing the unbelieving faces of the other guests is worth the effort.

In any case, I was more than a little proud of my first sausages, which I produced with a new caulking gun from the home improvement store. The sausage bug quickly infected friends and acquaintances and we meet every once in a while to make sausages and, of course, eat them.

Whoever picks up and browses through this book will quickly see that you can easily create your own "perfect sausage" and have a lot of fun as well.

Karsten "Ted" Aschenbrandt,
May 2011

Beloved
Bratwurst

The oldest known source
that mentions a sausage is
Homer's *Odyssey*.

> **And like a man before a great blazing fire**
>
> **Quickly turns to and fro a goat's stomach full of fat and blood,**
>
> **And is very eager to have it roasted,**
>
> **So Odysseus tossed from side to side,**
>
> **Pondering how he might put forth his hands upon the shameless wooers.**
>
> –Homer's *Odyssey*, book 20, verse 25

A goat's stomach filled with fat and blood is thus the first hint at some kind of food very similar to bratwurst. This description doesn't sound very inviting, but luckily the last 2,700 years have been used for further experimenting with this basic format.

But the Greeks weren't the only ones thinking of sausages; the Romans were keen on sausages as well. The following recipe is from the cook book De re coquinaria ("About the Art of Cooking") by Apicius, the oldest collection of recipes from the ancient Roman time—already there were more similarities to what we know as a sausage:

Pepper, caraway, savory, arugula, parsley, spices, bay laurel and liqvamen

[a spicy sauce made from fish]; add well-mashed minced meat and mix everything.

To this add more liqvamen, whole peppercorns, ample fat and nuts [e.g., pine nuts],

then fill the mix into a very thin casing.

This sausage is actually a smoked sausage and according to Master Apicius' directions, it can be roasted after being smoked for a short period.

At this point in the Roman lexicon, it was clear that "sausage" meant minced meat filled into casings. This was a way for small leftover pieces of meat to be used and combined into a new dish. The good home economics of this process made sausages very popular and the concept was embraced by many cultures around the world. Because of different tastes and dietary restrictions, sausage recipes developed in different directions and over time cult-like sausage regulations, unions, interest groups, and societies came into being.

Sausage Timeline:

3RD CENTURY	In ancient Rome the fried sausage loses its importance.
7TH CENTURY	Slavic people are said to have carried casings filled with mince meat when traveling.
11TH CENTURY	Guilds were created in towns and cities, and from these the first butchers appear.
1313	At the outer wall of the Moritz Chapel in Nuremberg, the *Nürnberger Bratwurst-glöcklein* ("Little Nuremberg Fried Sausage Bell," a restaurant) opens, and thus the Nuremberg Rostbratwurst is the first fried sausage mentioned in a historic text.
1370	In Esslingen, official regulations were created for the size of fried sausages.
JANUARY 20, 1404	*Thüringer Rostbratwurst* ("Thuringia fried sausage") is mentioned for the first time on a bill for the Arnstadt Virgin Monastery. The oldest known recipe is dated a year later.
1432	In Weimar, legislation is passed governing butchers and the purity requirements for all kinds of sausages.
1462	In Nuremberg, only butchers specializing in pork are allowed to produce bratwurst.
1470	In Esslingen, only pure pork is allowed for the production of bratwurst.
1498	The Coburger Bratwurst is mentioned for the first time on a menu for the George Hospital.
1573	The first sausage weighing 25 grams is fried in Nuremberg and remains a long-running success until today.
1600/1601	Butchers in Königsberg (Kaliningrad) create a giant sausage 2,200 feet (670 meters) long.

The oldest known recipe for bratwurst can be found in the state archive at Weimar. It stems from the "Rules for Weimar butchers," and is written down under §25. The bratwurst thus became official.	**1613**
Saint Mauritius becomes patron of Coburg and thus also of the Coburger Bratwurst (*Bratwurstmännla*, "little bratwurst guy").	**JUNE 1, 1622**
The *Gemerck-Zettul* is published, a standard reference for bratwurst cooks containing six recipes.	**1691**
With the *Thüringisch-Erfutisches Kochbuch* ("Thuringian-Erfurtian Cookbook") the first printed recipe for Thüringische Rostbratwurst is published.	**1797**
The *Nürnberger Bratwurstglöcklein* ("Little Nuremberg Fried Sausage Bell" restaurant) opens in Munich.	**1893**
During World War II, the Nuremberg Moritz Chapel, and thus also the *Nürnberger Bratwurstglöcklein,* are destroyed by allied bombers.	**1944**
March 18: The city council of Nuremberg decides on a binding recipe for the Nürnberger Rostbratwurst. April 15: The recipe is published in the official gazette of Nuremberg. The *Schutzverband Nürnberger Rostbratwurst* ("Society for Protection of the Nuremberg Rostbratwurst") is founded. The recipe for the Nuremberg Rostbratwurst is registered at the German patent office.	**1998**
July 15: "Nürnberger Bratwürste" and "Nürnberger Rostbratwürste" are protected by EU mark of origin. You can read about this in the *Amtsblatt der Europäischen Gemeinschaft* "Official Journal of the European Community" (decree no. 1257/2003). December 17: The "Thüringer Rostbratwurst" now also enjoys the protection by the European Union.	**2003**
February 18: Foundation of the society *Freunde der Thüringer Bratwurst e.V.* ("Friends of the Thuringian Bratwurst") May 28: The first German bratwurst museum opens in Holzhausen.	**2006**

When you look at this timeline, you can see that fried sausages have a long tradition. But the future prospects are not bad either because:

"As long as the world turns, the sausage will turn along with it."

SAUSAGE FACTS:

The German Bratwurst Museum is located in Holzhausen.

The name Bratwurst is not derived from the verb braten ("to roast") but from Brät ("meat") with which it is filled.

For the Super Bowl, the "Stadium Brats" are dyed the colors of the two opposing teams.

The longest fried sausage in the entire world measures almost 4 miles (5,888 meters). Bernhard Offner, master butcher of Landshut, Germany, produced this sausage on June 27, 1999, together with 16 assistants and apprentices. It took 9 hours and 16 minutes to fill the casing with nearly 2 tons (1,700 kilograms) of sausage meat. This took place in a barn that was customized for the record-breaking event.

At Cabo de São Vicente, in the sun of Portugal, on the southwestern-most point of Europe, there is a stand called "Last fried sausage before America".

Bratwurst.tv, a YouTube channel exclusively dealing with sausages, has been around since 2008.

Martin Luther, the church reformist, once ate a Thuringian bratwurst at a restaurant but couldn't pay for it. The innkeeper made a mark on a board with a piece of chalk to document that Luther still owed him money for the bratwurst. But Luther never paid for the bratwurst and thus not only Luther, but everybody who owes something to somebody in Germany is referred to as in der Kreide stehen ("standing in the chalk").

More than 20 million Thuringian sausages have been produced in the Duc-Viet sausage factory in Vietnam, a German-Vietnamese joint venture.

Johann Wolfgang von Goethe had Nuremberg Rostbratwurst delivered to Weimar by mail.

Hans IV. Stromer (1517–1592), a city judge in Nuremberg, was sentenced to lifelong imprisonment in a tower because of revealing secrets and vile language. As a patrician, he had one wish granted and that was to receive two fried sausages each day at the city's cost. This he endured for 38 years, then he jumped off the tower to his death. It is said that he ate almost 28,000 fried sausages during his imprisonment.

Machines
and Gadgets

MEAT GRINDER
SAUSAGE STUFFER
FOOD PROCESSOR
CASINGS
OTHER TOOLS

MEAT GRINDER The meat grinder is the most important machine for producing sausages at home. It simplifies the process significantly by cutting meat and fat into small pieces evenly and replaces the need for chopping or mincing tools. The heart of every meat grinder is the feed screw inside. It turns and presses the meat pieces against a perforated plate at the front of the machine. At the same time, mounted between the front of the feed screw and the perforated plate, a grinder knife with four blades rotates. Pieces of incoming meat are pressed against the perforated plate and chopped by the blades, which are rotating close to the plate. Pieces of meat are pressed forward by the meat from behind, leaving through the holes.

The hole size of the perforated plate determines the fineness of the minced meat. Plates range in designation from coarse to medium to fine with corresponding hole diameters. For the best results, look for small diameters, like 1/8". Plates also come in different "sizes," which describe the size of the whole disk— the usual size for an ordinary kitchen is #5.

Various meat grinder plates, blade, and feed screw

Feed screw, blade, and plate assembled alongside the collar for fixing the assembly to the meat grinder

Electric meat grinder with feeding pan—perfectly suited for sausage production at home

The simplest meat grinders can be obtained for about $30. With these units the feed screw is turned manually with a crank, and the machine is secured by screwing it to the countertop or a table. These meat grinders sometimes contain additional plates for making cookies.

**Simple meat grinder
mounted to a table**

Useful electric meat grinders can be purchased for $50 and up. An upper limit—as with all kitchen gadgets—does not exist. However, it is not advisable to go with the cheapest unit: with 10 pounds of meat and a broken meat grinder, Sausage Sunday can quickly turn into a nightmare. Thus you should always look for ample power when buying a meat grinder; the minimum being 1,000 watts!

For both manual and electric meat grinders, attachments for sausage stuffing are available. But these require the sticky, mixed ground meat to be pressed through the feed screw once again, whereby the ground meat can clog up the whole meat grinder. In addition, the meat warms up and the fat starts to become greasy. With manual meat grinders, it is difficult to provide a consistent supply of meat, and electric grinders only know "on" and "off." But for stuffing, "quick" and "slow" are more important. Better results and ease of use can be achieved with a sausage stuffer.

Tube for sausage stuffing

SAUSAGE STUFFER

A variety of sausage stuffers are sold commercially, but the basic principle is always the same: a cylinder is filled with minced meat, which is pressed through an outlet by means of a piston. A stuffing tube is mounted in front of the outlet and the casing is put over it. The meat is pressed into the casing, which then moves along, almost automatically. An "endless" sausage is created until the casing is removed from the device.

If you want to get a sense for whether sausage making is right for you, save your initial investment in equipment by improvising a bit. The cheapest solution is to buy a caulking gun from a home improvement store for stuffing sausages. These guns consist of an aluminum tube and a piston, which is pressed forward by means of the trigger. Just make sure to buy a closed system that will allow you to load a plastic bag of ingredients. The nozzle, of course, has to be cut open wide enough so the meat can flow out unhindered. Because this stuffing tube has a small-diameter nozzle, sheep casings, which have a similarly small diameter (caliber) are best suited.

The simplest version of a sausage stuffer: a caulking gun

Of course working with a real sausage stuffer is more flexible and comfortable. Here the piston is moved forward with a gear rod, wheel, and crank. This way the forward progress of the meat can be easily controlled and the stuffing speed regulated. The stuffing tubes on these machines can be exchanged, and usually a variety of the most-used sizes is already included, so that everything from small sheep casings to a big bratwurst caliber can be stuffed easily. Like meat grinders, sausage stuffers are available in all price categories; useful machines can be

The inside of a sausage stuffer, notice the hole where the sausage meat feeds to the stuffing tube

This sausage stuffer has to be mounted to a tabletop.

obtained for about $50 and up. You shouldn't necessarily choose the cheapest solution. The cylinder has to withstand a certain amount of pressure and thus ought to be made from metal. A massive gear rod and secure positioning are indispensable. Whether the cylinder is positioned horizontally or vertically is of less importance.

Gears on a manual sausage stuffer

Semi-professional sausage stuffer with various stuffing tubes for different calibers of casing

FOOD PROCESSOR

Indispensable for producing fine meat is the food processor. Slightly different from the meat grinder, which divides the meat into smaller pieces only coarsely, the food processor creates a real mash. This is done with an extremely sharp, rotating sickle-shaped blade that cuts through the meat cells at a speed of up to 3,000 rpm. The result is a texture like that of fine liverwurst or bologna sausage. Since the rotating knives create heat when running, ice or cold water is added to cool down the mixture. Otherwise the protein would clot and the meat would solidify. A food processor can certainly be the most expensive investment for making sausage as a hobby—a good, small food processor for the kitchen could be hundreds of dollars. When starting out with sausage making, most food processors with suitable functions can achieve good results. With any model it is important that the lid can be closed and locked securely, otherwise the rotating knives can cause severe injuries.

Small, tabletop food processor with a 4 1/4-cup (3 liters) capacity

Drive shaft and control panel of the food processor

Bottom left: Sickle-shaped blade, covered on one side

Bottom right: The drive shaft comes up through the center hole in the mixer.

It is the casing that distinguishes a sausage from a meatball; it provides the crunchy bite and keeps the juice inside the sausage. For the production of bratwurst hog and sheep casings are used, which are trimmed and cleaned after slaughtering and butchering. Sheep casings are the most expensive and finest casings. They are also used as instrument strings, which indicates the strength of such a casing. For storing and preserving casings they are either put into brine or salted dry and sealed airtight; this way they can be kept in the fridge for months. Prior to processing, rinse the casing in cold water to remove the salt and then immerse in lukewarm water to make them smooth.

CASINGS

Dried and cured casings, bundled in various calibers

The thickness of the casings is organized into calibers. Here are the diameters in millimeters.

Thus the following sizes, suited for making bratwurst, are available for hog casings:	And for sheep casings:
	16/18
26/28	18/20
28/30	20/22
30/32	22/24
	24/26
	26/28

The usual quantity is often given in hanks. One hank is equivalent to 100 yards which, in turn, is the same as 91.44 meters.

Thus whoever buys 1 hank of 20/22 sheep casings receives 100 yards of sheep casings with a diameter of 20–22 millimeters.

OTHER TOOLS

Of course, for making sausages you need some additional items as well, which you should be able to find in every kitchen:

- ■ Cutting board and knife for cutting meat, fat, and herbs.
- ■ Precise digital scale for accurately weighing herbs (calibrated to weigh subdivisions of 0.5 grams).
- ■ Kitchen scales for weighing the meat.
- ■ Bowls and appropriate receptacles for mixing the meat with herbs and spices and for soaking the casings.
- ■ Spatula for scraping out sausage stuffer and bowls.
- ■ Kitchen twine or butcher's string for tying off the ends of the casings.

With these few additional tools, it is possible to produce pretty and delicious sausages yourself. If you have a vacuum sealer, the sausages can also be vacuum packed and frozen. They can be thawed quickly in lukewarm water, which means you are well prepared for the spontaneous barbecue.

But the most important additional tool in your kitchen is an enthusiastic helper. Having an extra set of hands simplifies the task and, of course, it is much more fun to make sausages together.

The most important tools for sausage production

From Meat to Sausage

GRINDING

To start, you need a meat grinder. You might think this is obvious, but since no pork belly or shoulder fits into the grinder whole, the first steps in sausage production are executed with a knife. Basically, the pieces of meat have to be cut small enough to fit into the funnel of the meat grinder.

Skin, gristle, and bones should not find their way into the meat grinder. Also, the meat should be cut into cubes rather than strips with long fibers.

The following photos show the step-by-step process:

An entire pork belly with ribs...

...and skin.

Cut into the periosteum next to the ribs...

...loosen the rib bones...

...and pull them out with your hand.

Cut the belly into thick slices...

...so that it's easier to loosen the skin from the fat...

...and pull the meat with the fat from the skin.

Cut the strips with the skin removed into equally-sized cubes.

The cubed pork

The meat used for making sausages should have a lot of natural flavor. Thus muscle groups the living animal used extensively are particularly suited. This includes, the neck, belly (with each drawing of breath the breast and ribcage move), and shoulder. As a result, however, there are many tendons and connective tissue located in these cuts. These can be hard on a meat grinder, so we help it by cutting the meat into walnut-sized pieces. By doing this we are pre-processing the strong fibers in the tendons and connective tissue.

A pork neck...

...is first cut into evenly sized...

... slices...

...then into strips...

...and finally...

...into cubes.

For grinding raw bacon from the belly or back, freeze it slightly prior to grinding. The protein will be harder, the fat less greasy, and overall the pieces will be easier for the meat grinder to cut. If the frozen bacon is cut into cubes with a length of about 3/8" (1 cm) per side and then mixed with the meat cubes prior to grinding, the mixture will be well processed by the meat grinder, and the bacon and meat will be distributed more evenly. Herbs and spices can also be added to the mixture now and incorporated evenly.

After grinding, kneading always follows. The ground meat has to be kneaded until it becomes sticky, which gives the sausage its stiffness and prevents it from falling apart. You can add the spices during this process if they were not already added prior to grinding. Make sure there are no clumps of spice and that herbs and spices are distributed evenly within the ground meat.

Kneading is best done manually and with a sufficiently large bowl. Things are easier, of course, if you have a mixer with suitable kneaders. Manual kneading is not very tiresome, but the meat has a temperature of about 40–43°F (4–6°C), which in the long run can lead to cold hands…

**Meat grinder
with cubed
meat and spices**

**Feeding pan
with pusher**

Distribute spices evenly in the ground meat.

Copious kneading creates stickiness.

PROCESSING To create finely ground meat from coarse meat, a food processor is quite efficient. The meat grinder prepares the protein for the quickly rotating sickle-shaped blades, which further break and divide the meat fibers. The food processor now can cut a smooth and homogeneous meat mash from the ground meat, which is then used for creating fine bratwurst. The friction created by the sides of the blades as they slice through the meat at up to 3,000 rpm generates heat. But heat can reverse the stickiness obtained by kneading the ground meat, thus it should not heat up to more than 55–60°F (12–15 °C) in the food processor. This warm up can be prevented by placing well-cooled ground meat into the processor. In addition, you can add about 15% of crushed or pulverized ice, so the mixture can be cut without problems and without heating up too much. Measure the temperature by briefly sticking a meat thermometer into the ground meat.

Place the ground meat into the food processor.

Close the lid securely...

...and lock it.

The processor will only start if the lid is locked.

The finished meat mixture

STUFFING

While grinding and processing is mostly done by a machine, stuffing requires a bit more skill and manual dexterity. First of all, the cylinder of the stuffer is filled as compactly as possible with the meat mixture—make sure to remove air bubbles. If the cylinder is not stuffed compactly enough, air bubbles in the sausages will rupture during frying. The meat should always be stuffed immediately after kneading, otherwise it will harden and pressing it through the stuffing tube will be difficult. Place the rinsed casing over the moistened stuffing tube. Here the entire length of the tube can be used, which keeps the casing on the tube so you won't have to continue placing the casing over the front of the tube again and again. Slip the casing over the tube carefully without twisting it; any rupture will cause the meat to escape. At the tip of the nozzle let the casing hang off 2–2.5 inches (5–6 cm); this will become one of the sausage ends. Make sure that this end is not tied up yet, because the air inside the stuffing tube still needs to escape.

When the casing is placed over the stuffing tube, slowly and carefully move the piston until the air in the tube has escaped completely and the meat starts to appear. Now the casing can be knotted and tied up and stuffing can start. The piston moves evenly and consistently, and the meat leaving the front pulls the casing along. Here you have to make sure that the sausage is always led away from the stuffer in a straight line and without kinks and that the casing is moving along smoothly and by itself. Don't fill the sausage too tightly because then it can't be tied into individual sausages later on. About 2 inches (5 cm) before the end of the casing, stop the piston and knot the second end of the sausage. Now you should have a loosely folded sausage about 8–16 feet (2.5–5 m) long with two knotted ends lying in front of you. Perhaps this is a little too big for the grill or pan, so tie it off into smaller sausages!

With thumb and forefinger, press the meat away a bit at the ends of the sausages. If they were filled too tightly, they will rupture. Then tie off every second sausage with about 5 turns. If every single sausage were tied, the one before would become untied again each time. At the places the sausages were tied, cut them off with scissors. This completes the production of bratwurst—the way they are known and loved by everyone.

To better see the individual work steps, they are shown once more with step-by-step photos:

Fill the cylinder of the sausage stuffer with ground meat...

...stuff it compactly without creating air bubbles.

Slip the moistened casing on to the tube.

Carefully turn the crank so the casing starts to fill...

...an "endless" sausage is created...

...which is tied off at the end.

Measure the sausage to the desired size...

and tie it off by twisting.

From the initial "endless sausage," many small, perfect sausages are created...

41

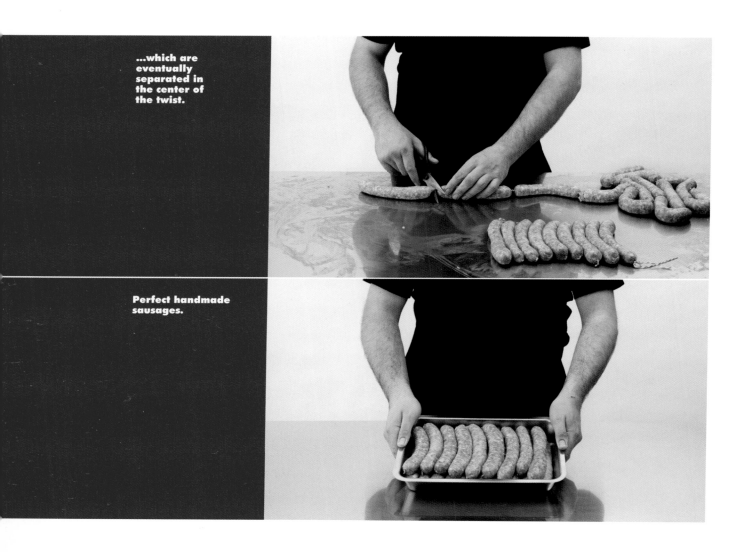

...which are eventually separated in the center of the twist.

Perfect handmade sausages.

SCALDING

Scalding helps preserve the sausage and makes it easier to use the bratwurst during meal preparation. The sausages are cooked in boiling water, which makes them ready to be eaten afterwards. The grill or a frying pan is then only responsible for providing the roasted flavor and color.

The most important aspect of scalding is managing the proportion of salt in the boiling water; it must be the same as that of the sausage. If it is too high, moisture is drawn from the sausage and the sausage dries up; if it is too low, the sausage draws water and ruptures during roasting later on.

The correct amount of salt can easily be translated from the amount of salt in the recipe to the amount to be used for the water.

The rule of thumb for the duration of scalding is:

■ Scalding duration at 170–175°F (76–80 °C) is 1.5 minutes per millimeter of the casing's caliber; thus a sausage with a diameter of 30 mm needs about 45 minutes.

■ When scalding sausages, cooking them more gently leads to a better consistency and crispness in the final product. Therefore the temperature shouldn't exceed 175°F (80 °C).

■ The best approach is to monitor the core temperature with a meat thermometer. When the core temperature of the sausage, measured at the thickest point, reaches 158°F (70°C), the scalding process is finished. To avoid pricking holes into the sausage, push the thermometer carefully into the sausage at the tied end.

Fresh, fine bratwursts ready for scalding.

Fresh vs. Scalded –

The Biggest Differences

Are all bratwursts created equal? Absolutely not!

Apart from the different recipes, the differences are mainly due to the consistency of the ground meat and the diameter of the casing.

FRESH OR RAW BRATWURST

Fresh or raw bratwurst is made of, as the name already implies, fresh ground meat. The best results are achieved when ground meat is purchased and processed on the same day. The reason for this is that grinding the meat creates a much larger surface area for bacteria and other germs than exists on the whole cut of meat. Therefore making sausage with the freshest product available is important to making sure the sausage is also fresh.

left: coarse, raw bratwurst
right: fine, scalded bratwurst

left: fine, roasted bratwurst
right: coarse, roasted bratwurst

Meat for **raw** bratwurst in general is ground more coarsely. Generally the sausage contains pieces of meat the size of a pea.

The creation of **fresh** bratwurst in your in-home sausage factory is less laborious and well-suited for first attempts. Getting the meat to a fine consistency in a food processor is not necessary and scalding is omitted: the meat is only ground, mixed with spices, kneaded, and then filled into casings. Of course, you don't have to eat the sausages on the very same day; they can be frozen easily.

On the other hand, frying and roasting raw sausages is more difficult than cooking scalded sausages because they have to be cooked to temperature on the inside without being charred on the outside.

SCALDED BRATWURST

Since the meat inside the scalded bratwurst takes on a firmer consistency when heated, these sausages are harder or rather stiffer and lighter in color than raw ones. Canned sausages, bratwurst wrapped in film, or vacuum-sealed bratwurst in general are always scalded. This means, they are already cooked and ready to eat and only have to be browned. Thus the regulations for ground meat don't apply here, and these sausages are all the more suitable for gastronomy and commerce. Besides their ability to be stored for a longer period of time, they are easier to roast or fry and also still keep their shape after a couple of hours on the food warmer. The latter, unfortunately, can be seen at many hot-dog stands where the "cook" often produces ahead of sale and then simply keeps the sausages warm.

Thus you can be confident that the bratwurst at the fair or in the stadium is always a scalded one.

THICK OR THIN?

Of course there are "rules" for all kinds of bratwurst with respect to their thickness and length, but quality meat always tastes good, regardless of whether the sausage is thick or thin, short or long. Here only one's personal taste is the final authority.

Commerce dictates the various thicknesses at which the casings are sold—the calibers. For normal bratwurst, hog casings with a bit larger caliber or diameter are recommended. For Nürnberger or thin sausages, in general sheep casings are suitable. These are a bit finer in structure and of a smaller caliber. When considering the thickness of the casing and the length of the sausage, preparing scalded or fresh sausages doesn't matter here.

The Perfect Grilled Sausage

HEAT
APPEARANCE
CAUTION! HOT!
TIPS FOR GRILLING

Once you have a completed bratwurst, the icing on the cake, the final polish, and ultimate upgrade to sausage aristocracy is to cook it on the grill.

A bratwurst from the grill just tastes the best. Simply imagine if at the next county fair the large, customary grill were replaced by a pan for heating sausages and steaks. Everything would quickly drown in its own fat and crisp sausages would be things of the past—a catastrophe.

THE GRIDIRON IS TO THE BRATWURST WHAT THE LID IS TO THE POT!

But why is this the case? Why does a sausage from the grill taste different than one from the pan? Which type of grill is most effective: gas, charcoal, or electric? How do I avoid charring the outside of the sausage while its raw on the inside? These are questions which every sausage fan surely has asked himself/herself at least once already.

One thing up front: In principle, a sausage can be prepared on any grill, but the results will be different. These differences are mainly with respect to raw sausages. Pre-scalded sausages are easier to grill and forgive many mistakes, but with respect to crispness and taste, they don't reach the quality of a fresh, raw sausage. So a pre-scalded sausage that has spent two hours on the food warmer of a hot dog stand doesn't look much different than a sausage that was just roasted. But after two hours in the same conditions, a fresh bratwurst would have withered into a shriveled little mockery of a sausage.

HEAT Heat is heat, right? Not at all. You need dry heat to grill sausages because the skin reacts immediately to the surrounding moisture. If there is too much moisture, the skin shrinks and becomes soft instead of crisp. Good electric and gas grills should have a lid which keeps the heat inside, efficiently preventing excessive loss of heat. However, the lid also holds moisture inside. This is great for maintaining the juiciness of meat, but not so great for sausage casings—the moisture makes the skin soft. Thus my recommendation for the perfect barbecue sausage is a charcoal grill. The infrared radiation of the glowing charcoal is dry, neutral with respect to taste, and hot enough that grilling without a lid is possible. And the most important benefit is that the sausages achieve crispiness.

APPEARANCE A sausage from the pan is brown on two sides, but that is all. A grilled sausage is brown on all sides and has the characteristic grill marks. Only these stripes brand the sausage as a grilled sausage. The best grill marks can be achieved with gridirons made of cast iron or thick stainless steel. These materials retain heat especially well and convey it to the sausage without cooling down themselves.

CAUTION! HOT! The best way to the perfect grilled sausage is the correct configuration of your grill's heat source (e.g., gas burner, charcoal, etc.) The trick is to create a hot and a cold zone. This is easy with the charcoal grill: stack the charcoal on one half of the grill and leave the other half empty. With a gas or electric grill activate the burner or heating elements accordingly. If your grill only has one burner or heating element, use a warming rack as a cold zone.

The sausage can now be grilled on the direct heat. If it turns too dark or flames appear, you can simply pull it into the safe, cold zone where it can finish cooking without burning up. Of course, the opposite works just as well: cook the sausage in the cold zone then sear it in the hot zone until it is crisp, brown, and pretty.

GRILLING TIPS

- Don't start grilling until the charcoal is covered with a white layer of ashes.

- Only use well-proven charcoal starters, never use alcohol!

- The best accessory is a charcoal chimney or chimney starter. Let the gridiron heat up after putting it in place.

- Always grill with a hot zone and a cold zone.

- Turn the sausages with tongs: a fork injures the skin and lets the juices escape.

- Some sausage experts put pine cones, pieces of wood, grape vines, or herbs into the embers. This provides an aromatic smoke.

With these tips and a bit of knowledge about sausages, I wish you lots of success as you pursue the perfect grilled sausage!

Here is a step-by-step photo guide to perfectly grilling sausage—from lighting the fire to the cooking process.

There can be no embers without flames.

The charcoal chimney
slowly starts to work...

...the embers burn their
way upwards...

...finally covering
the charcoal pieces
on top with a layer
of ashes.

Dump the glowing coals into the grill...

...and, using heat-resistant tongs...

...stack the coals on one side of the grill. Now you can start grilling.

Here are three fine and three coarse sausages placed directly on top of the charcoal.

Be sure to turn the sausages in a timely manner.

Move the browned sausages into the cold zone where they will finish cooking in the indirect heat.

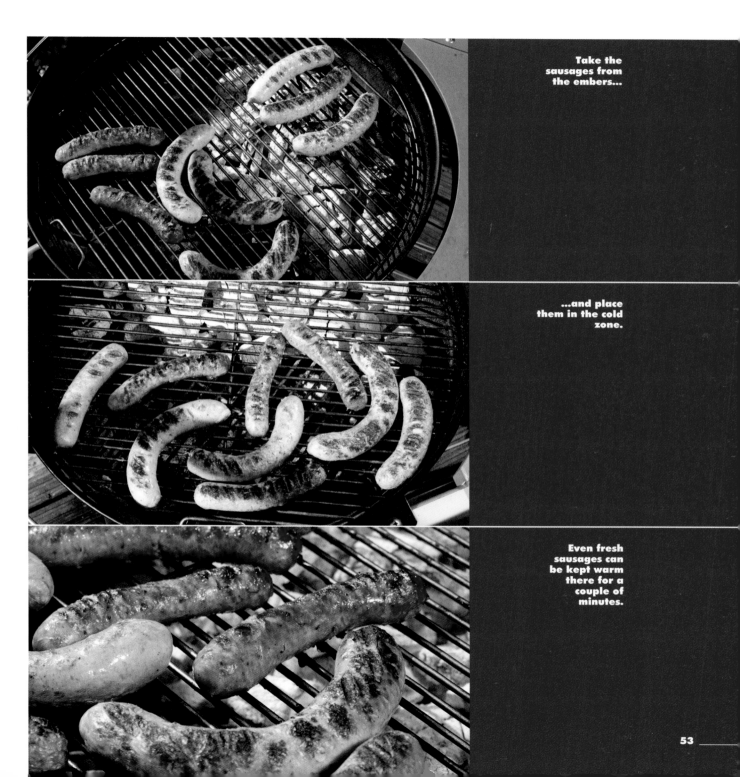

Take the sausages from the embers...

...and place them in the cold zone.

Even fresh sausages can be kept warm there for a couple of minutes.

THE CLASSICS:
LOCAL SAUSAGE RECIPES

SPECIAL AND
EXOTIC SAUSAGES

Sausage Recipes

The Classics – Local Sausage Recipes

The classic German sausages are usually named after their place of origin and can always be found in many variations. But there is one thing they all have in common: they are all very tasty!

THÜRINGER ROSTBRATWURST

Makes 5½ lbs (2½ kg) of sausage		
MEAT:		
4½ lbs (2 kg)	pork shoulder	
1⅛ lbs (500 g)	beef neck	
SPICES:		
3 T. (55 g)	salt	
2 t. (5 g)	white pepper, finely ground	
1 t. (1½ g)	mace	
½ t. (2½ g)	cumin	

PREPARATION:

Grind the meat in a meat grinder with a #8 plate.

Add all other ingredients and mix well until the mass becomes sticky.

Fill into sheep casings and divide into sausages of about 3–3½ oz (80–100 g) each.

NÜRNBERGER ROSTBRATWÜRSTL

Makes 5½ lbs (2½ kg) of sausage

MEAT:

3⅓ lbs (1½ kg)	pork shoulder
2¼ lbs (1 kg)	raw bacon

SPICES:

2¾ T. (50 g)	salt
2⅓ t. (5 g)	black pepper, finely ground
1½ t. (2½ g)	marjoram, dried
1⅛ t. (2½ g)	nutmeg
2⅛ t. (2½ g)	onion flakes

PREPARATION:

Cut the meat into cubes.

Add the other ingredients and mix it into a smooth mash with the food processor.

Fill into thin sheep casings and tie them off to a weight of ¾ to 1 oz (20 to 30 g) each.

COBURGER BRATWURST

Makes 5½ lbs (2½ kg) of sausage

MEAT:

2¼ lbs (1 kg)	pork shoulder
2¼ lbs (1 kg)	pork belly without skin
1⅛ lbs (500 g)	beef neck

SPICES:

2¾ T. (50 g)	salt
1 T. (7½ g)	white pepper, finely ground
2 t. (3 g)	mace
⅔ t. (3 g)	lemon peel powder (also lemon powder)
2	eggs

PREPARATION:

Grind the meat in a meat grinder with a #8 plate.

Add the spices and eggs and mix until the mass becomes sticky.

Fill into hog casings made from the serosa (outer skin of the intestines) and twist off to a weight of 3–3½ oz (80–100 g) each. If you can't get serosa casings, you can also use normal sheep casings.

FRÄNKISCHE BRATWURST

Makes 5½ lbs (2½ kg) of sausage

MEAT:

1¾ lbs (800 g)	beef neck
1¾ lbs (800 g)	pork shoulder
2 lbs (900 g)	pork belly without skin

SPICES:

2¾ T. (50 g)	salt
2⅓ t. (5 g)	black pepper, finely ground
1 t. (2 g)	allspice
1⅛ t. (2 g)	mace
1⅛ t. (2 g)	ginger powder
3 t. (5 g)	marjoram, dried

PREPARATION:

Grind the meat in a meat grinder with a #5 plate.

Add all other ingredients and mix everything well until the mixture starts to become sticky.

Fill into 20/26-caliber hog casings and twist off to a weight of 3–3½ oz (80–100 g) each.

REGENSBURGER BRATWURST

Makes 5½ lbs (2½ kg) of sausage

MEAT:

3⅓ lbs (1½ kg)	beef neck (use veal shoulder for a finer sausage)
1⅛ lbs (500 g)	pork neck
1⅛ lbs (500 g)	raw back bacon (Irish or Canadian) without skin

SPICES:

3⅓ T. (60 g)	salt
2 t. (5 g)	white pepper, finely ground
⅞ t. (1½ g)	ginger powder
¼ t. (1½ g)	coriander, finely ground
⅓ t. (1½ g)	lemon powder

PREPARATION:

Cut the meat and fat into cubes. Don't mix the pork neck with the beef and bacon.

Freeze the bacon slightly and meanwhile grind the pork neck in a meat grinder with a #8 plate.

Cut the bacon and beef into a smooth mash with a food processor, then mix it thoroughly with the spices and the pork neck.

Fill into sheep casings and twist off at a length of about 4 inches (10 cm).

RHEINLÄNDER BRATWURST

Makes 5½ lbs (2½ kg) of sausage

MEAT:

4 lbs (1⅞ kg)	pork neck
1½ lbs (700 g)	raw back bacon

SPICES:

3 T. (55 g)	salt
2½ t. (6 g)	white pepper, finely ground
⅓ t. (0.5 g)	mace

PREPARATION:

Cut the meat and bacon into cubes.

Freeze the bacon slightly and then cut it into a fine mash with the other ingredients.

Fill into hog casings of any size and twist them off to an approximate weight of 3½ oz (100 g).

FRANKFURTER BRATWURST

Makes 5½ lbs (2½ kg) of sausage	**MEAT:**	
	2¼ lbs (1 kg)	fresh, lean ham or pork back
	3⅓ lbs (1½ kg)	raw back bacon (or neck bacon)
	SPICES:	
	3½ T. (65 g)	salt
	2 t. (5 g)	white pepper, finely ground
	1½ t. (3 g)	paprika powder
	⅓ t. (2 g)	coriander, finely ground

PREPARATION:

Cut the meat into cubes and mix thoroughly with the spices.

Cover and put it into the fridge over night.

Continue cutting until the bacon is pea-size.

Fill into thin hog casings and twist off at a weight of 3–3½ oz (80–100 g) each.

PFÄLZER BRATWURST

Makes 5½ lbs (2½ kg) of sausage	**MEAT:**	
	2¾ lbs (1¼ kg)	pork neck
	2¾ lbs (1¼ kg)	pork belly without skin
	SPICES:	
	2¾ T. (50 g)	salt
	2⅜ t. (5 g)	black pepper, finely ground
	1⅛ t. (2½ g)	nutmeg
	½ t. (2½ g)	coriander
	2	cloves of garlic, mashed

PREPARATION:

Grind the meat in a meat grinder with a #8 plate.

Add all other ingredients and mix everything thoroughly until the mixture becomes sticky.

Fill into hog casings of caliber 20/26 and twist off at a weight of 3–3½ oz (80–100 g) each.

MÜNSTERLÄNDER MILCHBRATWURST

Makes 5½ lbs (2½ kg) of sausage

MEAT:
3⅓ lbs (1½ kg)	pork neck
1¾ lbs (800 g)	pork back
½ lb (200 g)	beef neck

SPICES:
3⅓ T. (60 g)	salt
3 t. (6 g)	black pepper, finely ground
1½ t. (2½ g)	mace

OTHER INGREDIENTS:
⅞ cup (200 ml)	milk

PREPARATION:
Grind the meat in a meat grinder with a #5 plate.

Add spices and the milk and mix everything thoroughly until the mixture starts to become sticky.

Fill into 20/26-caliber hog casings and twist off to a weight of 3–3½ oz (80–100 g) each.

OBERLÄNDER BRATWURST

Makes 5½ lbs (2½ kg) of sausage

MEAT:
3½ lbs (1⅔ kg)	pork shoulder
2 lbs (900 g)	pork belly without skin

SPICES:
2¾ T. (50 g)	salt
2 t. (5 g)	white pepper, finely ground
⅞ t. (1½ g)	mace
⅓ t. (1½ g)	lemon powder

OTHER INGREDIENTS:
⅜ cup (100 ml)	dry white wine (e.g., Riesling)

PREPARATION:
Cut the pork belly, freeze it slightly, then grind in a meat grinder with a #3 plate.

Cut the meat into cubes, place it in a food processor and mix it with the pork belly.

Add all spices and the wine and mix everything thoroughly until the mixture becomes sticky.

Fill into 20/26-caliber hog casings and twist off to a weight of 3–3½ oz (80–100 g) each.

SCHLESISCHE WEIHNACHTSBRATWURST

Makes 5½ lbs (2½ kg) of sausage		
MEAT:		
	2¼ lbs (1 kg)	veal shoulder
	1⅛ lbs (500 g)	pork back
	⅞ lbs (400 g)	raw back bacon
SPICES:		
	2¾ T. (50 g)	salt
	2 t. (5 g)	white pepper, finely ground
	2 t. (3½ g)	mace
	⅓ t. (1½ g)	lemon powder
	½ t. (2½ g)	seasoning (powdered bouillon or other prepared flavoring mix)
OTHER INGREDIENTS:		
	2½ cups (600 ml)	milk
	⅛ cup (30 g)	fresh onions, chopped

PREPARATION:

Cut the meat and bacon into cubes.

Freeze the bacon slightly, then mix it into a smooth mash in a food processor with the meat and other ingredients.

Fill into 30/32-caliber hog casings, twist off to a weight of about 5⅓ oz (150 g) and scald.

Slowly fry at low temperature and with lots of butter.

SCHWÄBISCHE BRATWURST

Makes 5½ lbs (2½ kg) of sausage

MEAT:

2¼ lbs (1 kg)	pork shoulder
2¼ lbs (1 kg)	pork belly

SPICES:

3⅓ T. (30 g)	curing salt
1⅔ t. (4 g)	white pepper, finely ground
2⅓ T. (4 g)	marjoram, dried
1⅛ t. (2 g)	mace
½ t. (2 g)	lemon powder

OTHER INGREDIENTS:

2⅛ cups (500 ml)	milk

PREPARATION:

Cut the meat and pork belly into cubes.

Freeze the pork belly slightly, then mix with spices, milk, and meat into a smooth mash in a food processor.

Fill into hog casings of any size, twist off at a length of about 4½ inches (12 cm) and scald.

WÜRZBURGER OR WINZERWURST

Makes 5½ lbs (2½ kg) of sausage

MEAT:

4½ lbs (2 kg)	pork shoulder
1⅛ lbs (500 g)	beef neck

SPICES:

2¾ T. (50 g)	salt
2 t. (5 g)	white pepper, finely ground
⅞ t. (1½ g)	mace
½ t. (2½ g)	cumin

OTHER INGREDIENTS:

⅜ cup (100 ml)	dry white wine from Germany's Würzburg region

PREPARATION:

Grind the meat in a meat grinder with a #8 plate.

Add all spices and the wine and mix thoroughly until the mixture becomes sticky.

Fill into sheep casings and twist off to a weight of 3–3½ oz (80–100 g) each.

STEIRISCHE ERDAPFELWURST

Makes 5½ lbs (2½ kg) of sausage

MEAT:

1⅛ lbs (500 g)	pork belly without skin
⅔ lbs (300 g)	beef neck
⅔ lbs (300 g)	dried meat

SPICES:

2¾ T. (50 g)	salt
2 t. (5 g)	white pepper, finely ground
1⅛ t. (2½ g)	nutmeg
2⅓ T. (4 g)	marjoram, dried
1½ T. (4 g)	thyme, dried
1½ t. (2 g)	savory, dried

OTHER INGREDIENTS:

2½ cups (400 g)	onions, chopped
2¼ lbs (1 kg)	potatoes

PREPARATION:

Grind potatoes, meat, and onions in a meat grinder with a #5 plate.

Add all other ingredients and mix everything well until the mixture starts to become sticky.

Fill into casings of size 30/32, twist off at a length of 6 inches (15 cm) and scald.

BERLINER CURRYWURST

Makes 5½ lbs (2½ kg) of sausage

MEAT:
4 lbs (1⅞ kg)	pork shoulder
1⅛ lbs (500 g)	raw back bacon

SPICES:
2¾ T. (50 g)	salt
2 t. (5 g)	white pepper, finely ground
2½ t. (5 g)	curry powder
2⅓ t. (5 g)	turmeric
1 t. (2 g)	cumin

OTHER INGREDIENTS:
⅞ cup (200 ml)	cream

PREPARATION:

Cut the meat and raw bacon into cubes.

Freeze the bacon slightly, then mix with spices, cream, and meat and process everything into a smooth mash.

Fill into hog casings of any size, twist off at a length of about 4 inches (10 cm) and scald.

HUNGARIAN BRATWURST

Makes 6⅔ lbs (3 kg) of sausage

MEAT:
4½ lbs (2 kg)	pork neck
1⅛ lbs (500 g)	pork belly without rind

SPICES:
2½ T. (45 g)	salt
2½ t. (6 g)	white pepper, finely ground
2⅓ t. (5 g)	paprika powder, medium hot
2½ t. (5 g)	curry powder

OTHER INGREDIENTS:
⅞ cup (200 ml)	cream
3	eggs, beaten well

PREPARATION:

Grind the neck in a meat grinder with a #8 plate and the belly with a #5.

Mix the spices and other ingredients with the ground meat and knead for about ten minutes.

Fill into 28/30 hog casings and twist off sausages with a length of about 6 inches (15 cm).

HESSISCHE BRATWURST

Makes 5½ lbs (2½ kg) of sausage	**MEAT:**	
	2¼ lbs (1 kg)	pork shoulder
	1⅛ lbs (500 g)	pork topside (inner leg)
	½ lb (250 g)	veal breast
	1⅔ lbs (750 g)	raw back bacon
	SPICES:	
	3 T. (55 g)	salt
	2 t. (5 g)	white pepper, finely ground
	1⅛ t. (2 g)	mace
	1⅛ t. (2 g)	ginger powder

PREPARATION:

Cut the meat and bacon into cubes.

Freeze the bacon slightly, then mix all ingredients together and grind in a meat grinder with a #2 plate.

Fill into thin hog or sheep casings and twist off to a weight of about 3–3½ oz (80–100 g) each.

Special
and Exotic Sausages

Sometimes, to produce a good sausage you can consider using spices and ingredients that, at first glance, are not seen as typical for sausages. Game, poultry, fish, and even crabs can be ground and filled into casings. As long as you stick to the basic rules, there are no limits to creativity.

WILD BOAR BRATWURST

Makes 5½ lbs (2½ kg) of sausage

MEAT:

2¼ lbs (1 kg)	wild boar shoulder
2¼ lbs (1 kg)	wild boar belly without skin
1⅛ lbs (500 g)	raw back bacon without skin from a domestic pig

SPICES:

2¾ T. (50 g)	salt
2⅞ t. (6 g)	black pepper, coarsely ground
2⅓ T. (4 g)	marjoram, dried
3⅓ t. (4 g)	rosemary, finely ground
⅔ t. (3 g)	cumin
⅞ t. (1½ g)	mace
2	cloves of garlic, mashed

Wild boar has a tendency to be rather lean, so use the belly of the beast and add back bacon from a domestic pig to make sure the sausage has enough moisture.

PREPARATION:

Grind the meat and bacon in a meat grinder with a #5 plate.

Add all other ingredients and mix everything thoroughly until the mixture becomes sticky.

Fill into 28/30-caliber hog casings and twist off sausages with a weight of 3–3½ oz (80–100 g) each.

SALSICCIA

Makes 5½ lbs (2½ kg) of sausage	The classic Italian Salsiccia, (pronounced "sal-seet-chia") gets its traditional flavor from fennel and red wine.

MEAT:

| 3½ lbs (1⅔ kg) | pork shoulder |
| 2 lbs (900 g) | Italian lardo or raw back bacon |

SPICES:

2¾ T. (50 g)	salt
3 t. (7 g)	black peppercorns
2½ t. (5 g)	fennel seeds
5	cloves
1⅛ t. (3 g)	cinnamon

OTHER INGREDIENTS:

3	cloves of garlic, mashed
1	chili pepper (medium hot), finely cut
1	bunch of fresh cilantro, finely cut
1 cup (250 ml)	red wine

PREPARATION:

Grind the meat and bacon in a meat grinder with a #5 plate.

Crush peppercorns, fennel seed, and cloves thoroughly with a mortar and pestle.

Mix all ingredients thoroughly until the mixture becomes sticky.

Fill into 28/30-caliber hog casings and twist off to a weight of 3–3½ oz (80–100 g) each.

LAMB MERGUEZ

Makes 5½ lbs (2½ kg) of sausage

MEAT:

5½ lbs (2½ kg)	lamb shoulder

SPICES:

2¾ T. (50 g)	salt
2⅓ t. (5 g)	black pepper, finely ground
¾ t. (3½ g)	cumin
½ t. (3 g)	coriander, finely ground
1 t. (2.5 g)	cinnamon
1⅔ t. (8 g)	harissa
2⅞ t. (6 g)	paprika powder
1 tsp (3 g)	garlic powderr

OTHER INGREDIENTS:

⅜ cup (100 ml)	olive oill

This Moroccan lamb sausage gets its red color from harissa and paprika. It should be grilled extra dark, almost black.

PREPARATION:

Grind the meat in a meat grinder with a #8 plate.

Mix all ingredients thoroughly, slowly adding in oil, until the mixture becomes sticky.

Fill the ground meat into sheep casings and twist off sausages of 3–3½ oz (80–100 g) each.

BEEF MERGUEZ

Makes 5½ lbs (2½ kg) of sausage

MEAT:

4½ lbs (2 kg)	beef neck
1⅛ lbs (500 g)	fat from beef

SPICES:

2¾ T. (50 g)	salt
2⅓ t. (5 g)	black pepper, finely ground
1½ T. (10 g)	paprika powder
1⅔ t. (3 g)	cayenne pepper
⅔ t. (3 g)	cumin
⅞ t. (2 g)	clove powder
1½ T. (4 g)	thyme, dried

OTHER INGREDIENTS:

⅜ cup (100 ml)	olive oil

In this merguez recipe, the traditional lamb is replaced by beef. The seasoning is a little more tame, but the overall flavor isn't affected. To punch it up a little, add a little more Cayenne pepper.

PREPARATION:

Grind the meat in a meat grinder with a #8 plate.

Mix all ingredients thoroughly until the mixture becomes sticky. While doing so, slowly add oil.

Fill the ground meat into sheep casings and twist off sausages of 3–3½ oz (80–100 g) each.

CHICKEN BRATWURST

Makes 5½ lbs (2½ kg) of sausage

This is a delicious sausage with reduced calories, but making it requires a few more steps. The chicken legs in this recipe need to be deboned first (chicken breast is not a suitable cut because it lacks fat). Because the amount of meat varies, the spice quantities are per 2¼ lbs (1 kg) of deboned meat.

MEAT:

11 lbs (5 kg)	chicken leg quarters

SPICES (PER 2¼ LBS [1 KG] OF MEAT):

22 g	salt
2.2 t. (5 g)	white pepper, finely ground
½ t. (1 g)	chili powder
⅓ t. (½ g)	mace
⅛ t. (½ g)	lemon powder

PREPARATION:

Remove the skin from the legs and debone the meat. Don't waste the fat, you'll need it to keep the sausages moist.

Grind the meat in a meat grinder with a #3 plate.

Add the spices and mix it thoroughly with the ground meat until the mixture becomes sticky.

Fill into sheep casings or thin hog casings and twist off sausages of 3 oz (80 g) each.

TURKEY BRATWURST

Makes 5½ lbs (2½ kg) of sausage

MEAT:

4 lbs (1⅞ kg)	turkey breast
1⅛ lbs (500 g)	smoked back bacon

SPICES:

55 g	salt
2 t. (5 g)	white pepper, finely ground
1⅛ t. (2 g)	marjoram, dried
1 t. (2 g)	nutmeg

OTHER INGREDIENTS:

⅞ cup (200 ml)	milk

This sausage is seasoned like a traditional bratwurst, but the ground meat is created from poultry. The bacon provides a back bone for bratwurst flavor here.

PREPARATION:

Grind the meat and bacon in a meat grinder with a #3 plate.

Add all other ingredients and mix them thoroughly until the mixture becomes sticky.

Fill into sheep casings and twist off sausages of 3–3½ oz (80–100 g) each.

DUCK BRATWURST

Makes 5½ lbs (2½ kg) of sausage

MEAT:

6	duck legs
4	duck breasts

SPICES:

3⅓ t (20 g)	salt
2¼ T. (20 g)	curing salt
2⅓ t. (5 g)	black pepper, finely ground
2 t (4 g)	five-spice powder
3 T. (5 g)	marjoram, dried
1⅛ t. (2 g)	mace

Here is a different way to roast duck. Don't remove the skin from the breast. That and the tasty leg meat give this sausage a really nice duck flavor.

PREPARATION:

Debone the duck legs and grind the meat and the breast meat in a meat grinder with a #3 plate.

Carefully mix the meat with the other ingredients and knead until the mixture becomes sticky.

Fill into sheep casings and twist off sausages of 3–3½ oz (80–100 g) each.

APPLE AND ONION BRATWURST

Makes 5½ lbs (2½ kg) of sausage

Apples harmonize well with sausage meat. So why not add some to your next batch of sausage stuffing? The calvados intensifies the apple flavor.

MEAT:

2¼ lbs (1 kg)	pork shoulder
2 lbs (900 g)	turkey breast fillet
1⅓ lbs (600 g)	raw back bacon

SPICES:

2¾ T. (50 g)	salt
1⅓ t. (2½ g)	cayenne pepper
½ t. (2 g)	cumin
½ t. (1 g)	allspice, finely ground
1½ T. (4 g)	thyme, dried
2⅔ T. (10 g)	parsley, finely cut
2	medium-sized onions

OTHER INGREDIENTS:

⅜ cup (100 ml)	calvados
1⅔ cups (100 g)	apples, dried

PREPARATION:

Soak the apple pieces in calvados; in the meantime, cut the bacon into cubes and freeze slightly.

Grind meat, onions, and apple pieces in a meat grinder with a #3 plate.

Add the remainder of the ingredients and mix everything thoroughly until the mixture becomes sticky.

Fill into 28/30-caliber hog casings and twist off to a weight of 3–3½ oz (80–100 g) each.

RAMSONS* GRILLER

Makes 5½ lbs (2½ kg) of sausage

MEAT:

2¼ lbs (1 kg)	pork neck
2¼ lbs (1 kg)	pork belly without skin
1⅛ lbs (500 g)	beef neck

SPICES:

2¾ T. (50 g)	salt
3⅓ t. (10 g)	celery salt
2 t. (5 g)	white pepper, finely ground
2½ t. (2½ g)	thyme, dried
½ cup (25 g)	parsley, finely cut
⅓ cup (25 g)	ramsons, finely cut
⅞ t. (1½ g)	mace

This recipe won Winning Sausage in the Bratwurst with Side Dish category at the German barbecue championship in Gotha/Thuringia May 2010.

PREPARATION:

Grind the beef and pork neck in a meat grinder with a #4 plate.

Grind the pork belly in a meat grinder with a #2 plate.

Add all other ingredients and mix them thoroughly until the mixture becomes sticky.

Fill into thin hog casings or serosa and twist off to a length of 6–8 inches (15–20 cm) each.

*Ramsons (*Allium ursinum*) are a type of wild garlic very similar to ramps (*Allium tricoccum*), which can be used as a substitute.

TROUT BRATWURST

Makes 5½ lbs (2½ kg) of sausage

FISH:

4 lbs (1⅞ kg)	trout fillets, fresh
1⅛ lbs (500 g)	trout fillets, smoked

SPICES:

2½ T. (45 g)	salt
2 t. (5 g)	white pepper, finely ground
½ t. (2½ g)	lemon powder
2⅔ T. (10 g)	parsley, finely cut
1⅓ T. (3½ g)	thyme, dried

OTHER INGREDIENTS:

⅞ cup (200 ml)	cream

Fish in a bratwurst? Why not! The smoked trout fillets are key to the great flavor of this sausage.

PREPARATION:

Debone the fresh trout fillets and grind in a meat grinder with a #3 plate.

Chop the smoked fillets with a fork and mix with the minced trout.

Add spices and cream and knead until the ingredients are evenly distributed.

Fill into sheep casings and twist off to a length of 4 inches (10 cm).

SHRIMP BRATWURST

Makes 5½ lbs (2½ kg) of sausage

This is a variation on a recipe for shrimp bratwurst that was first made in Sankt Peter-Ording, Germany in 2004.

MEAT:

3½ lbs (1⅔ kg)	pork neck
⅔ lb (300 g)	pork belly without skin
⅞ lb (400 g)	shrimp, parboiled

SPICES:

2¾ T. (50 g)	salt
2 t. (5 g)	white pepper, finely ground
2⅔ T. (10 g)	chervil, fresh
2½ t. (5 g)	curry powder
1 t. (2½ g)	chili powder

OTHER INGREDIENTS:

⅞ cup (200 ml)	milk

PREPARATION:

Grind meat and pork belly together with the shrimp in a meat grinder with a #3 plate.

Add spices and milk and knead the mixture thoroughly.

Fill into sheep casings or thin hog casings and twist off into 4-inch (10 cm) sausages.

ARGENTINEAN CHORIZO

Makes 5½ lbs (2½ kg) of sausage

MEAT:
3⅓ lbs (1½ kg)	pork shoulder
1⅛ lbs (500 g)	raw back bacon
1⅛ lbs (500 g)	beef neck

SPICES:
1⅔ T. (30 g)	salt
2 t. (5 g)	white pepper, finely ground
2⅞ t. (6 g)	paprika powder
4 t. (4 g)	oregano, dried
2 t. (1.5 g)	bay leaves, powdered

OTHER INGREDIENTS:
2 T. (30 ml)	vinegar from red wine
⅞ cup (200 ml)	red wine, dry
2	medium-sized onions, chopped
4	cloves of garlic, mashed
	olive oil

This well-known paprika sausage is best served fresh from the grill.

PREPARATION:
Sweat the onions in a bit of oil and let them cool down.

In the meantime, grind meat and bacon in a meat grinder with a #5 plate.

Add spices, garlic, wine, and vinegar, then mix everything thoroughly until the mixture becomes sticky.

Fill into 26/28-caliber hog casings and twist off into 4-inch (10 cm) sausages.

A sausage is very tasty, but it is not a complete meal. Typically a sausage nestles into a bun as a great, quick snack between meals. But there are many creative recipes that go above and beyond this tradition and allow the sausage to shine in more substantive dishes.

Recipes with Sausage

SAUSAGE BALLS WITH POTATO CHIPS

4 servings

These simple ingredients combine nicely to create a dish that is great to serve as a party snack. The mango ragout provides an exotic touch.

INGREDIENTS:

4	fresh, coarse bratwursts (e. g., the Pfälzer on page 59)
1	ripe mango
⅜ **cup (100 ml)**	curry ketchup
1⅛ **lbs (500 g)**	sweet potatoes
2 T.	olive oil
2 T.	coriander leaves, chopped
	curry for decoration
	pepper
	salt

PREPARATION:

Peel the mango and cut one half of the fruit into cubes.

Puree the rest of the pulp and mix with coriander, mango cubes, and ketchup. Add salt and pepper to taste.

Peel the sweet potatoes, cut them into thin slices, oil them, and place them next to each other on a baking tray covered with parchment paper.

Bake in the oven on the middle rack for 15–20 minutes at 400°F (200°C).

While the potatoes are in the oven, squeeze the sausage filling out of the casings and roll them into small balls. Roast them in some oil for about 10 minutes until they are well-done.

Salt the potatoes slightly, put some mango ragout on top and add one sausage ball each. Sprinkle curry powder on top and serve warm.

BRATWURST WITH BEER SAUCE

4 servings

Though it is a tradition, brats don't always need to be served with mustard. This beer sauce is a great accompaniment for a spicy bratwurst and goes well with a side of fried potatoes or roasted mashed potatoes.

INGREDIENTS:

4	coarse bratwursts, (e.g., the Rheinische on page 58)
2⅛ cups (500 ml)	dark or malt beer
4	gingerbread cookies
	paprika powder
	pepper
	salt
	oil

PREPARATION:

Roast the bratwursts in a bit of oil, take them out of the pan, and keep warm. Reserve the rendered fat.

Crumble the gingerbread cookies into the rendered fat and cook together with the beer. Let it cook until everything has dissolved and the sauce has achieved the desired consistency.

Add salt, pepper, and paprika to taste and serve with the sausages.

WHITE CABBAGE WITH BRATWURST

4 servings

Bratwurst with sauerkraut is a rather universal dish. But combining sausage with white cabbage is a really delicious variation. Bacon, potatoes, and onions turn this into a hearty winter meal.

INGREDIENTS:

4	scalded bratwursts, cut into slices ¾ inch (2 cm) thick
1¾ lbs (800 g)	white cabbage, cut into strips
1⅛ lbs (500 g)	potatoes, cut into cubes
¼ lb (100 g)	bacon cubes
1	Spanish onion, finely cubed
1 cup (250 ml)	vegetable stock
⅞ cup (200 ml)	cream
	pepper
	salt
1 T.	marjoram, dried
	nutmeg

PREPARATION:

Sautee the bratwurst pieces together with the onion cubes and the bacon until the onions become translucent, then stir in the marjoram.

Place alternating layers of white cabbage, potatoes, and bratwurst into a casserole dish and add salt, pepper, and nutmeg to taste.

Fill up the casserole dish with the vegetable stock and cream and cook in the oven at 350°F (180°C) for 45 minutes.

SAUSAGE ROLLS

4 servings

The German name for this dish is *Bratwurst im Schlafrock*, which literally translates to "bratwurst in a nightgown." Since this "wrapped" sausage can easily be eaten without utensils, it makes for a great party snack.

INGREDIENTS:

10–20	scalded bratwursts, depending on size (e.g., the Nürnberger on page 56)
8	sheets of frozen puff pastry, already thawed
8	slices of bacon, serrano ham, or boiled ham, depending on your taste
8	slices of mild cheddar cheese
1	egg yolk

PREPARATION:

Gently roll out the sheets of puff pastry.

Wrap one slice of ham and one of cheese around the sausages, then place on the puff pastry. Wrap the dough around the sausage and slightly moisten the ends to be "glued" with the egg yolk. Press the ends gently with a fork.

Bake the rolls on parchment paper for about 25 minutes at 350°F (180 °C).

Serve hot or chilled, depending on taste.

BELGIAN SAUSAGE-PANCAKE SANDWICHES

4 pancakes

These potato pancakes filled with sausage meat and apple sauce appear to be a typical German meal. But actually they were created by a Belgian named Bart Mus. It just so happens that "apple sauce" in German is *Apfelmus*. A coincidence?

INGREDIENTS:

2	coarse bratwursts (e.g., the Thüringer on page 55)
12	medium-sized potatoes, peeled
3	medium-sized onions, finely cubed
4 T.	flour
2	eggs
8 T.	apple sauce
	pepper
	salt
	oil

PREPARATION:

Shred the potatoes, then add salt and pepper to taste.

Add onions, eggs, and flour and mix everything well. If the mixture becomes too loose, add some more flour.

Bake eight pancakes of equal size on one side in lots of oil, then take them out of the pan.

Squeeze the meat out of the sausage casings and shape four patties the same size as the potato pancakes. Cook them briefly on both sides in the pan.

Spread apple sauce on each of the pancakes with the unbaked side down and put a patty on four of them. Then put a second pancake on top with the uncooked side pointing upwards.

Now carefully put the sausage pancakes into the pan and cook until brown on the outsides.

APPLE-BRATWURST BREAD

4 servings

This dish is similar to a German *Schmandkuchen*, a cake made with sour cream, but is prepared with bratwurst. The combination of apples and bratwurst provides the extraordinary taste.

INGREDIENTS:

4	scalded bratwursts, cut into pieces
1⅛ lbs (500 g)	bread dough, available at the bakery or as a baking mixture
1⅛ lbs (500 g)	curd
⅞ cup (200 g)	sour cream
5	eggs
3 T.	sugar
4	apples, Braeburn or Boskoop, cut into wedges

PREPARATION:

Roll the dough to a thickness of ¼ inch (5 mm) and place it covered on a baking tray lined with parchment paper. Let the dough rise for about one hour.

Beat the eggs together with the sugar, then mix with the sour cream and curd until the mixture is smooth.
Spread the mixture evenly on the bread dough.

Place the apple wedges and sausage on top of the spread and bake for about 40 minutes at 350°F (180°C).

Serve warm or chilled, whichever you prefer.

STUFFED BRATWURST

4 servings

For stuffing, scalded sausages just over an inch (3 cm) in diameter are best suited. Crème fraîche and cheese keep these sausages very juicy. And the bacon helps to keep the sausage together.

INGREDIENTS:

4	thick, scalded bratwursts
1	medium-sized onion, cubed finely
2 T.	butter
2 T.	parsley, finely cut
2 T.	chives, cut into small rolls
2 T.	crème frâiche
¼ lb (100 g)	Swiss or emmentaler cheese, grated
8	slices of bacon
	pepper
	salt

PREPARATION:

Cut a groove down the length of the sausage. Make sure not to cut through the entire sausage. The ends and the outside of the sausage should stay intact.

Slightly brown the onion cubes in the butter and allow them to cool down.

Mix herbs, crème frâiche, and cheese with the onions, fill the sausages and wrap them with two slices of bacon each. Secure the bacon with toothpicks.

Roast them in the oven for about 15 minutes or grill in indirect heat until the bacon is crunchy. If using a grill, make sure it has a lid.

BRATWURST STRUDEL

4 servings

This delicacy features sausage wrapped up neatly in strudel dough. The meat adds spice, the cabbage makes it juicy, and the strudel dough provides a crunchy wrap.

INGREDIENTS:

4	sheets of strudel dough
4	scalded sausages to taste
2	medium-sized onions, finely cubed
¼	white cabbage, cut into fine strips
2	cloves of garlic, finely chopped
½ **cup (125 ml)**	cream
2	eggs, well beaten
⅓ **lb (150 g)**	Emmentaler cheese, grated
	pepper & salt
¼ **t.**	cumin
	clarified butter for roasting the sausages
5 T.	butter, melted
	breadcrumbs

PREPARATION:

Roast the bratwursts in clarified butter and allow them to cool down. Leave the fat in the pan.

Sautee onions and garlic in the bratwurst fat until soft, then add the cabbage and allow it to simmer for another 10 minutes. Let it cool.

Cut the sausage into thin slices, mix with the cabbage, cream, eggs, cheese, and spices to taste. If the mixture is too thin, you can bind it with some breadcrumbs.

Place sheets of strudel dough on top of each other while spreading the liquid butter over each of the sheets.

Spoon the sausage mixture onto the dough and wrap it. Leave the corners uncovered but brush butter on them. Then roll the strudel to an equal thickness and brush with the rest of the butter.

Bake in the oven at 350°F–400°F (180–200°C) for about 35 minutes.

SAUTEED BELL PEPPER WITH NÜRNBERGER ROSTBRATWÜRSTL

4 servings

**Here the bratwurst is the supporting actor in the pan.
Fine, scalded sausages like the Nürnberger on
page 56 are ideal.**

INGREDIENTS:

12	Nürnberger Rostbratwürstl, (page 56)
1 each	yellow, green, and red bell pepper with stem, core, and seeds removed and the rest cut into cubes
1 cup (200 g)	rice
2	leek stalks, cut into rings
2 T.	paprika powder
⅞ cup (200 ml)	vegetable stock
⅜ cup (100 ml)	crème frâiche
	pepper
	salt
	oil

PREPARATION:

Cook the rice according to the package, then put aside.

Grill or roast the sausages. In the meantime, sautee the bell peppers and leeks
in a big pan with a bit of oil until everything is soft. Add salt and pepper to
taste and mix in the paprika powder.

Add the vegetable stock and let it simmer.

Add rice and Nünrberger and heat everything well.

Decorate with a dab of crème frâiche and serve.

CHICKEN BRATWURST WITH BRUSSELS SPROUTS

4 servings

Chicken bratwursts and Brussels sprouts combine to create a mild, but hearty and pleasing meal.

INGREDIENTS:

4	chicken bratwursts (page 69)
1¾ lbs (800 g)	potatoes, peeled
1¾ lbs (800 g)	Brussels sprouts, rinsed and drained
2	large tomatoes
3 T.	parsley, chopped
⅞ cup (200 ml)	milk, warm
4 T.	butter
	pepper
	salt
	nutmeg
	oil

PREPARATION:

Remove 2–3 pretty outer leaves from each of the Brussels sprouts and put them aside. Cut the rest of the sprouts into halves.

Cut the potatoes to the same size as the Brussels sprouts and cook together in water with ample salt at moderate heat for 15 minutes.

In the meantime, remove the core of the tomatoes, cut the fruit into cubes, and heat the milk.

Roast or grill the bratwursts for 6–10 minutes, depending on their thickness.

Strain the sprouts and potatoes, but reserve the water and put it back on the stove. Add milk and butter to the potatoes and mash them well. While doing so, add nutmeg, salt, pepper, and 2 T. of parsley.

Heat the leaves of the Brussels sprouts in the boiling potato water for about one minute, then chill them.

Prior to serving, decorate the mashed potatoes with the leaves, cubed tomatoes, and the rest of the parsley, then serve together with the sausages.

BRATWURST QUICHE

4–6 servings

This savory dish revises the statement about real men eating quiche. Serve it with a cold beer and it won't matter if it's quiche or not. The sausage for this is fresh and made of one piece, not twisted off.

INGREDIENTS:

1⅛–1⅔ lbs (500–600 g)	bratwurst, not twisted off
½ cup (125 g)	butter
2 cups (250 g)	flour
4	eggs
⅔ cup (150 g)	crème frâiche
1 bunch	parsley, cut into rolls
4 T.	coarse Dijon mustard
½ t.	cumin
	pepper
	salt

PREPARATION:

For the dough, mix the flour with 1 t. of salt.

Melt the butter, let it cool down a bit, then beat it together with one egg. Add to the flour mixture and turn the mixture into a smooth dough. Shape the dough into a ball, cover with plastic wrap and put into the fridge for about 1 hour.

In the meantime, beat the rest of the eggs and while doing so, add mustard, parsley, and crème frâiche. Add cumin, salt, and pepper to taste.

Take the dough out of the fridge and roll out. Place it into a greased springform pan. Leave a border of about ⅜–¾ inch (1–2 cm) and pierce several times.

Place the sausage onto the dough in a spiral and pour the egg-mixture on top.

Bake in the oven at 350°F (180°C) for 40–50 minutes.

Cut into slices and serve immediately.

LEEK PIE WITH BRATWURST

4 servings

This leek pie is a great dish for a potluck dinner.
The size can easily be adjusted to the number of guests.

INGREDIENTS:

4	scalded bratwursts, cut into pieces of 1 cm length
1½ **cups (350 ml)**	vegetable stock
2	leek stalks, cut into rings
1	red bell pepper
5 T.	butter
3 T.	flour
¼ **lb (100 g)**	Emmentaler cheese, grated
	pepper
	salt

PREPARATION:

Cut the pepper into small cubes and cook together with the leeks in vegetable stock for about 10 minutes. Afterwards strain, but keep the stock.

Melt the butter in a pot and mix with the flour. Gradually add the vegetable stock and reduce to a sauce. Remove from the stove and stir the cheese into the mix.

Fill vegetables, sauce, and sausages into a casserole dish in several layers while generously adding salt and pepper. Then bake for about 25 minutes at 400°F (200 °C).

STUFFED MINI BELL PEPPERS

4 servings

**Mini bell peppers are as mild as their larger cousins.
To spice things up a bit, substitute jalapeños for the bell peppers.**

INGREDIENTS:

4	coarse bratwursts to taste
12	mini bell peppers
⅓ cup (125 g)	mozzarella cheese
1	egg, separated into white and yolk
2	tablespoonfuls of Herbes de Provence
	pepper
	salt

PREPARATION:

Cut the stems from the peppers and remove all membranes and seeds.

Cut the mozzarella into small cubes and mix with the herbs and the egg yolk.
Beat the egg white until stiff and fold in.

Squeeze the sausage meat from the casings and fill each of the peppers with
about 1 T. of meat, then cover with the egg, cheese, and herb mixture.

Bake for about 15 minutes at 400°F (200 °C) until the peppers are soft and the
cheese is brown and tasty.

APPLES AND BEANS WITH BRATWURST

4 servings

The acidity of the apple is a foil to the richness of the sausage. When considering sausages, the best option for this recipe is the Fränkische or a bratwurst of similar taste. For more apple flavor, use the Apple and Onion-Bratwurst on page 71.

INGREDIENTS:

4	bratwursts to taste
1⅔ cups	white beans, drained (about one 15.5 oz can)
2	apples (e.g., Braeburn), without core and cut into slices
2	medium-sized onions, chopped
2	cloves of garlic, chopped
4 T.	butter
1⅓ cups (300 ml)	vegetable stock
2 sprigs	fresh rosemary
	oil
	pepper
	salt
	sugar
	lemon juice

PREPARATION:

Sautee the onions and the garlic in a bit of oil for about 5 minutes.

Add the beans and the vegetable stock plus salt, pepper, and a squirt of lemon juice, then cook for about ten minutes over medium heat.

Fry the apple slices in butter together with the rosemary. While doing so, add some sugar and allow the apples to caramelize. At the same time, roast or grill the sausages.

Puree the beans and serve together with the apple slices and sausages.

PASTA WITH SALSICCIA

4 servings

It can hardly be any easier: without much effort you can quickly conjure up an authentic Italian meal.

INGREDIENTS:

5	salsiccia (page 67)
1⅛ lbs (500 g)	pasta (e.g., tagliatelle)
3	medium-sized onions, finely cubed
3	cloves of garlic, finely chopped
¾ cup (100 g)	pine nuts
1⅓ cups (300 ml)	white wine
⅜ cup (100 ml)	vegetable stock
	pepper
	salt
1 T.	dried oregano
	nutmeg
	olive oil
2 T.	butter

PREPARATION:

Squeeze the sausage meat from the casings and roll into small balls. Heat olive oil and butter and fry the sausage balls on all sides over medium heat.

Add onions, pine nuts, and garlic and continue frying until the onions are soft and becoming translucent.

Add wine and vegetable stock and let it simmer uncovered for 40 minutes until it has turned into a thick sauce.

Cook the pasta according to instructions on the package, pour the sauce on top and serve hot.

TAGLIATELLE WITH GORGONZOLA SAUCE AND BRATWURST BALLS

4 servings

The strong flavor of the gorgonzola is best accompanied by a light sausage that is not too salty and a sip of good white wine. For pasta, farfalle or gnocchi also work very well for this dish.

INGREDIENTS:

1 ⅛ lbs (500 g)	tagliatelle
4–5	mild, fresh bratwursts
¼ lb (100 g)	gorgonzola
5⅓ oz (150 g)	mascarpone (a little more than half of an 8-oz container)
⅜ cup (100 ml)	vegetable stock
a splash	cream
½ lb (200 g)	chanterelles or forest mushrooms
	pepper

PREPARATION:

Squeeze the sausage meat from the casings and shape into small balls. Brown the sausage in a bit of oil, then remove and keep warm.

Fry the mushrooms in the sausage oil, let them shrink, add salt and pepper.

In a second pan, melt gorgonzola and mascarpone together and add a tad of cream to enhance the consistency of the sauce. Cook the pasta al dente.

Strain the pasta, add the bratwurst balls and mushrooms, and mix everything with the sauce.

KRINGELBURGER

4 burgers

Finally, sausages served in a bun! But this dish is prepared in a different style for a change. Enjoy a cheeseburger and bratwurst at the same time. What more could you want?

INGREDIENTS:

4	relatively thin, fresh bratwursts about 10 inches (25 cm) in length
8	slices of camembert
¼ lb (100 g)	arugula or mixed salad, rinsed (one 5 oz bag)
1	medium-sized red onion, cut into rings
2	pickles, cut into slices
	Dijon mustard
	spicy ketchup
4	burger buns or normal rolls

PREPARATION:

Roll the sausages into a spiral and secure with a long wooden spit of sufficient length. Without the spit, they don't keep their round shape during roasting.

Roast or grill the sausage spirals.

Meanwhile put mustard, ketchup, and salad greens on the bottom buns.

When the spirals are finished, remove the spit and place the bratwurst on top of the greens.

Top with onion rings, pickles, cheese, and the other half of the bun.

SAUERKRAUT AND SAUSAGE ROLL

4 servings

Sauerkraut is one of the classic side dishes accompanying bratwursts; here a roll is added. A bit of harissa elevates the seasoning, and the roll sops up the juices.

INGREDIENTS:

4	bratwursts to taste, about 150 g each
4	rolls
⅔ lb (300 g)	sauerkraut, ready-to-eat (a little more than half of a 16-oz bag)
⅔ cup (150 g)	crème frâiche
⅔ cup (150 g)	cream
2 T.	harissa
1 T.	sugar
2 T.	butter
	pepper
	salt
	oil

PREPARATION:

Melt the sugar and caramelize a bit, then add the butter and let it melt.

Add the sauerkraut and simmer for five minutes in the caramelized butter, then mix with harissa, cream, and crème frâiche. Add salt, pepper, and oil to taste. Let simmer uncovered for about 15 minutes.

In the meantime, roast or grill the sausages and cut the rolls.

Place sauerkraut and one sausage on each roll and serve.

PUTTES

4–6 servings

Puttes, also called *Kesselkuchen* ("cauldron cake") is a hearty potato casserole from Rhineland. There are several variations.
Here, of course, is a version with bratwurst.

INGREDIENTS:

4½ lbs (2 kg)	potatoes
2	big onions
2	eggs
4–6	bratwursts,
	(e.g., the Rheinische on page 58)
⅓ lb (125 g)	Speckwürfel
	pepper
	salt
	nutmeg
about 4 T.	oil

PREPARATION:

Grate the potatoes and the onion finely.

Fold in the eggs and bacon cubes and add salt, pepper, and nutmeg to taste.

Fill a sufficiently big casserole dish with the mixture up to about ⅜ inch (1 cm) and put the sausages on top.

Pour the remaining mixture on top to cover the sausages.

Add some oil on top and bake at 400°F (200 °C) for 45–60 minutes.

BRATWURST-BREAD KEBABS

4 skewers

This is a fun dish for an outdoor party. When assembling the skewers, you can either wrap the sausage around the bread or the bread around the sausage.

INGREDIENTS:

4	scalded bratwursts (e.g., the chicken bratwurst on page 70)
1	loaf of white bread
1 T.	Herbes de Provence
	pepper
	salt
	olive oil
	skewers

PREPARATION:

Cut two sausages across into round pieces that are ¾ inch (2 cm) long and two sausages lengthwise into strips that are ⅛ inch (3–4 mm) thick.

Remove the crust of the white bread and cut the bread lengthwise into slices about ¾ inch (2 cm) thick.

Cut two slices into cubes of about ¾ inch (2 cm) and cut another two slices into strips of about ⅛ inch (4–5 mm) thick.

For the first skewer pattern use the sausage pieces and bread strips; the strips of bread should be wrapped around the sausage pieces. The second pattern should be done the opposite way.

Mix herbs, salt, pepper, and olive oil well and brush the skewers with the mixture.

Bake in the oven at 320°F (160°C) for about 15 minutes until the bread is crunchy.

BLAUE ZIPFEL

4 servings

The name Blaue Zipfel, or Saure Zipfel, ("blue" or "sour ends" [of sausages]) derives from the wine and vinegar in which the sausages are scalded. Fränkische or Thüringer bratwursts are best for this dish.

INGREDIENTS:

4	Fränkische bratwursts (page 57), about 6⅓ oz (180 g) each
4	medium-sized onions, cut into strips
2	carrots, cut into thin slices
1	tablespoonful of mustard seeds
1 T.	black peppercorns
10	juniper berries
⅜ cup (100 ml)	white wine vinegar
⅞ cup (200 ml)	dry white wine
2	cloves
3	bay leaves
	salt
	sugar
3⅛ cups (750 ml)	water
2 T.	parsley, chopped, for decoration

PREPARATION:

Crush peppercorns, mustard seeds, and juniper berries slightly with mortar and pestle, then put aside.

Boil water, wine, and vinegar; add all other ingredients with the exception of sausages and parsley and allow them to simmer for another 10 minutes.

Put the sausages into the hot broth and let them simmer for 10–15 minutes.

Take the sausages out of the broth, decorate with a bit of parsley, and serve together with bread and mustard.

BRATWURST DUMPLING

4 servings

This is a dumpling like you've never seen before.
In fact it is just one large dumpling that isn't cooked in
water but baked in a casserole dish. Depending on taste,
you can also add cut vegetables (e.g., pieces of tomato
or zucchini).

INGREDIENTS:

4–5	coarse bratwursts
1⅔ lbs (750 g)	dough for dumplings
1	big onion, finely cubed
2	cloves of garlic, finely chopped
2	eggs
2 T.	fresh thyme, finely chopped
2 T.	fresh rosemary, finely chopped
1 T.	curry
½ t.	chili powder
½ lb (200 g)	firm mozzarella, grated
	pepper
	salt

PREPARATION:

Mix all ingredients, except the sausages, and half of the mozzarella thoroughly
and add salt and pepper to taste.

Grease a casserole dish and evenly distribute half of the dough in it.

Squeeze the sausage meat out of the casings, shape into balls, and place them
on the dough. Cover with the remaining dough half.

Cover the casserole dish with aluminum foil and bake at 350°F (180°C) for 30
minutes. Then, uncover the dish, sprinkle the remaining mozzarella on top of
the dumpling and bake for another 15 minutes.

BRATWURST WITH SWEETHEART CABBAGE

4 servings

INGREDIENTS:

4⅓ cups (300 g)	sweetheart cabbage (pointed cabbage), cut into fine strips
3	carrots, julienned
4	bratwursts (e.g., the Rheinische bratwurst on page 58)
1 T.	butter lard
1	medium-sized onion, finely cubed
1⅓ cup (300 ml)	vegetable stock
3 T.	crème frâiche
2 T.	coarse Dijon mustard
	pepper
	salt
	sugar

PREPARATION:

Roast the sausages in clarified butter, then remove them from the pan. Keep the fat.

Cook the sweetheart cabbage together with the carrots in boiling salt water for 3 minutes and cool rapidly.

Sautee the onion in the sausage fat, add the cabbage and carrots, and heat them up.

Cool the mixture down by adding the vegetable stock; fold in crème frâiche and mustard, and add spices to taste.

Place the sausages back into the pan, heat them up and serve with the cabbage mixture.

MERGUEZ WITH TOMATO-POLENTA

4 servings

Polenta does a great job of soaking up delicious sausage juices. This dish is balanced with acidity and freshness provided by the tomatoes and basil.

INGREDIENTS:

4	merguez sausages (page 68)
1 cup (150 g)	Polenta
3⅓ cups (800 ml)	vegetable stock
⅞ cup (200 ml)	dry white wine (e.g., Riesling)
3 T.	butter
4	vine tomatoes
8	cherry tomatoes, cut into quarters
½ sprig	basil, cut into fine strips
¼ lb (100 g)	parmesan, half cut into thin slices and half grated
	pepper
	salt
	olive oil

PREPARATION:

Cook the vegetable stock together with the wine, butter, and 2 T. of olive oil. In the meantime, remove the core from the vine tomatoes and cut them into small cubes.

Mix in the polenta cornmeal and bring to a boil again. Then add the tomato cubes and salt and let it simmer uncovered for about 15 minutes over medium heat.

Grill the sausages. Roasting would also work, but the best results come from grilling merguez.

Mix the grated parmesan with the polenta and add spices to taste.

Plate the polenta and merguez with the cherry tomatoes, sliced parmesan, and basil, then serve.

SAUSAGE SHASHLIK

4 servings

These kebabs are not cooked in shashlik sauce, but they are peppered with vegetables and come from the grill. They are easy to prepare and add a pop of color to any cook out.

INGREDIENTS:

4	scalded bratwursts of your choice
2	medium-sized, red onions, cut into eights
1	yellow bell pepper, cut into 1 ⅛-inch (3 cm) pieces
1	zucchini, cut into ¾-inch (2 cm) slices
8	small potatoes, peeled and cooked
8	slices of bacon
	oil
	pepper
	salt
	skewers

PREPARATION:

Cut the bratwursts into ¾-inch slices.

Wrap a piece of bacon around every potato.

Skewer the ingredients, alternating items, with sufficiently large spits and brush with a bit of oil.

Grill evenly on all sides until the vegetables are done and the bacon is crunchy.

BRAISED CUCUMBER AND BRATWURST SOUP

4 servings

**The fresh cucumbers harmonize well with the spiciness of the brat-
wurst. If scalded bratwursts are used, cut them into slices; with
fresh bratwursts, squeeze the sausage meat out of the casing and
roll it into small balls.**

INGREDIENTS:

4–5	bratwursts
2	cucumbers
⅔ cup (150 g)	crème fraîche
2 T.	coarse Dijon mustard
4¼ cups (1 liter)	vegetable stock
3 T.	chives, diced small
	pepper
	salt
	oil

PREPARATION:

Peel the cucumbers, cut them into halves lengthwise, remove the seeds, and cut
into cubes. Put aside.

Roast the bratwurst pieces or balls in a pot with some oil until they have a nice,
brown color, then take them out.

Sautee the cucumber cubes in the hot sausage fat for about 5 minutes over
medium heat. Add salt and pepper to taste.

Add stock until the cucumber pieces are well covered, then fold in the mustard.
Let simmer for about 10 minutes until the cucumbers are soft.

Add the sausages and heat everything once more briefly while folding in the
crème fraîche.

Serve hot.

Appendix

SAUSAGE RECIPES FROM A–Z

RECIPES WITH SAUSAGES

GLOSSARY

back or green bacon	**Pure, white bacon fat without any meat**
Brät	**German term for sausage meat, the actual filling of the sausage, which gives the bratwurst its name.**
caliber	**unit of measurement for the thickness of sausage casings**
calvados	**apple brandy from the Normandy region of France**
cohesion	**The breaking apart of the protein chains makes the sausage meat tough and sticky; it coheres and becomes firm**
core thermometer	**electric thermometer with sensor for measuring the temperature inside cooking meat**
coriander powder	**ground coriander seeds**
cumin	**dried and ground seeds of the herb Cuminum cyminum**

GLOSSARY

curing salt	mixture of table salt, sodium nitrate, sodium nitrite, and potassium nitrate for preserving meat and sausages
five-spice powder	Asian mixture of star anise, Sichuan pepper, cinnamon, fennel seeds, and cloves.
food processor	machine for finely cutting food
hank	American unit for measuring sausage casings; 1 hank = 100 yards (91.44 m)
harissa	spice paste or powder from Morocco
lemon powder	dried and ground lemon peel
mace	ground blossoms of nutmeg
serosa	protective skin around the intestines, contains fat
spice nests	uneven distribution of spices within the sausage meat

Karsten "Ted" Aschenbrandt was born in Bonn, Germany, in 1971 and still remains true to the Rhineland. His family instilled an enthusiasm for food. He developed a love for cooking good meat, especially grilling.

Ted has turned grilling into his profession. He plans and leads grill and bbq seminars for various manufacturers and specialist retailers. During the colder months his calendar is filled with product tests, preparing content for various (grilling) media, and leading seminars for dealers. Catering and working at trade fairs complete his annual schedule.

For 5 years, Ted has been competing successfully in the World BBQ Association's (WBQA) championships. Together with his team, he was able to bring home a couple of victories.

Ted's books and recipes always follow the motto "keep it simple." Home chefs will find his recipes easy to understand and prepare. They are flexible and can be easily adapted to suit diverse palates. Ted's dishes also invite experimentation; basically, nothing can go wrong.

ABOUT THE AUTHOR

...FER COOKING TITLES

www.schifferbooks.com

Cooking Together: Having Fun with Two or More Cooks in the Kitchen. G. Poggenpohl. Everyone pitches in with this cookbook designed for multiple cooks in the kitchen. More than 30 recipes have two sets of instructions: for each cook or team of cooks. There's a game, puzzle, or riddle with each recipe to guarantee a fun time in the kitchen for all.

Size: 8 1/2" x 11"   36 color photos   80pp.
ISBN: 978-0-7643-3647-8   hard cover $19.99

Pure Steak. Steffen Eichhorn, Stefan Marquard, and Stephan Otto. Star cook Stefan Marquard, meat expert Stephan Otto, and German grillmaster Steffen Eichhorn present 39 extraordinary steak recipes. From exciting twists like Ribeye Stirred and Not Shaken and Sirloin Meets Scallop to traditional offerings like Garlic Steak and Filet Mignon, this soulful cookbook is ideal for all meat lovers.

Size: 8 1/2" x 11"   84 color images   136pp.
ISBN: 978-0-7643-3927-1   hard cover $29.99

Pure BBQ! Steffen Eichhorn, Stefan Marquard, & Stephan Otto. Powerhouse German foodies Steffen Eichhorn, Stefan Marquard, and Stephan Otto tackle grilling and smoking everything from oysters to mini beer keg suckling pigs. Through many hours spent BBQing and tasting, the trio has developed 34 excellent recipes including pierced perch, melon and halibut skewers, beech plank salmon, and antipasti, as well as classics for the smoker—pulled pork and beef brisket.

Size: 8 1/2" x 11"   47 color photos   128pp.
ISBN: 978-0-7643-4013-0   hard cover $24.99

Schiffer books may be ordered from your local bookstore, or they may be ordered directly from the publisher by writing to:

Schiffer Publishing, Ltd.
4880 Lower Valley Rd.
Atglen, PA 19310
(610) 593-1777; Fax (610) 593-2002
E-mail: Info@schifferbooks.com

Please visit our website catalog at **www.schifferbooks.com**
or write for a free catalog.

Printed in China